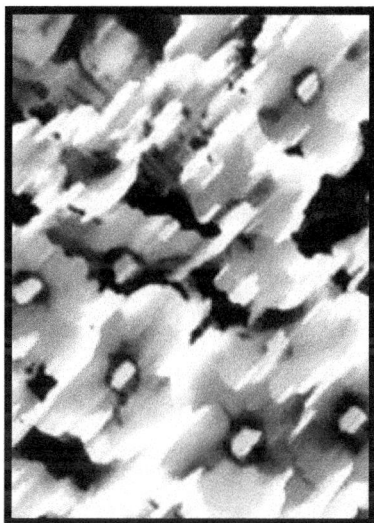

Lovely Faze

Owen Patterson

BREVIS Publishing ■ Chicago

A collection of poetry
Characters
Pressed together
Syllable sounds and words
Turn of phrase
Eclectic and mundane
Incoherence
Dreams of comprehension
Thoughts Lovely, and Fazed

Titles by Owen Patterson

The Dis-condition of Ease (prose fiction, 2015)

Lovely Faze (poetry, 2017)

Stars at Naught (poetry, 2018)

Jaded (poetry, 2018)

Fear Naught
The Junk Drawer of Poetry (poetry/prose, 2019)

See online book reviews at *Windy City Reviews*

BREVIS Publishing, Chicago, IL USA; 2018 **EDIT** x5.7
ISBN: 978-0-9964834-3-8 (BREVIS)
        9781974014996 (CS/KDP)

Formatting by Owen Patterson
Cover design by "Pica"; Edmund Barca
Back cover image- Lucille and Owen Patterson

Special Thanks:
Yasmeen Patterson Ahmad, Edmund Barca Gaylord,
Florentina Lona, Seréz Faunantino
Thanks for your advice and help.

Karin Janine

"What Truly Shines

Will Always Shine"

-F.L.

CONTENTS

I don't know a lot about anything
I like images
I like sound
I like touch
I can tell a story, or two

the human condition from birth

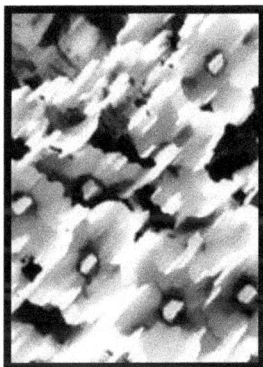

Lovely

...turn of phrase

Beautiful The Day

Absorb your tears
Salts coalesce, mingle
Season the bland
Beautiful the day
Radiant
Your conception

Just Awhile

I count less the count
Day to day waylay
'Til never
Then 'til now
Waiting 'til whenever
Eternity
The same as forever
I'm tired
No mind close eyes?
If only the sun would rise
And bring your smile
I'll wait just awhile

Ease and Repose

The star in my sky
Shines so bright
Its warmth
Puts me at ease

When weary
It guides me to
Peaceful Repose

This Serene Drama

In the night sky
Rose one beauty
Her light fell slow and deliberate
Beckoning Earth with gentle caresses
Earth answered with Wind
He whirled through the trees
Parted the clouds
That Beauty could be viewed entirely
This night
This heaven
Played only this serene drama

She wanted for tenderness
His heart touched
He longed to be close
Wherefore he rushed here and there
He rushed high
To meet her with kiss
Spinning in heaven
He was born a star
There they remain
Twins
For all eternity
This Serene Drama

Heaven and Earth
Wind and Star

I Remember

To dream of spring in September
I remember that time
A warm embrace
Left open
The circle not yet closed
The grass grows
Beneath my back
Lilac
Face to the sun
African violet softens the breeze
Bringing the homeland
To my home
That time I remember
Your hair swept across
My chest
We caress
Softness becomes us
Grace tickles the flesh
Love tingles the spine
That time
I remember
Dreaming of spring
In September

Spring dazzles my eyes
The joy of birth and rebirth
Summer heat fires my core
And deepens my hue
Fall is awesome
September skies overcast
Bristling with energy
In winter
I am mindful
Leafless trees
And biting cold
I dream of spring
As if it were heaven

I remember you

Oh Beautiful Sunshine

Open eyes
Look into darkness
My room

The sun sleeps

Through sheer cloth
Moonlight filters
In my eyes
Crystals dancing
Stirring chilled air

Oh beautiful sunshine
Rise
Touch my face
With warm kisses

Oh beautiful sunshine
Radiate
Spark life

Please rise
Touch my face
With warm kisses

16

Faze

...dreams of comprehension

What Remains

He always hated that painting
When his wife left
He took a blade to the canvas
He slashed it to bits
He stomped it with boot
He burned it to ash
His wife did not return
He always hated that painting
He still sees it
Whenever he passes
That empty wall

Once Again Love

Once again
Love raises its evil head
Swinging 'round
Gazing for last
Upon that precious stone

Once again
Love, that devilish
I feel the arrow fall
Upon that precious ruby
Shattering it

Strange what comes to mind
As I fade
I recall the gentle hand
That once caressed
Now holds the bow and the quiver

Collage

Above
Chameleon sky
Changing shade
With every stride
Of that woman I call
Collage

A shimmering elusive
A mirage
Or, is she real?

Intrinsic conclusive
Confuse inducive
Ambiguous
Ambitious
Provocative

Her deeper shades
Make men white
Frivolous lighter shades
Even whiter
They age with pursuit

She's sexy
Presence powerful
Unnerving
Sensual
Hence you will
Fall
Upon her call

It is difficult to recover
After

Collage

Missed Inspiration

I sat cleansing
Opened my heart
Down came the rain
The earth was scarred and arid
Water fell through the cracks
Pooling
Deep rumbling

I opened my mind
A wellspring flowed
I was almost there
But I forgot my cup
Waters slipped through my fingers
Back into the sand

Next time I'll know

Speak "Human"

Island patch
I sat... in despair
Transistor... whistles and cracks
Chuckles and taunts
I tried
But I don't speak "Machine"
I listened
But I don't understand
Though I began... to hope
Transistor cup potent
Brimming with empty
Could still be filled
Overflowed with "Human"

Memes... and posts, and coda

/mēm/ noun

elements of behaviors, concepts, or ideas passed culturally by means of duplication, imitation, or facsimile

Florentina Lona

The Nature of Earth is pristine.

I am abstract
Observe, engage, interpret
Think of me as you will
I can never say who I am
That would defeat the purpose

_F. L._

"I'll take it to the grave."

Joy should always be
the sustenance of youth.

F. L.

Even artists, who make their own paints using pigments from the Garden, plagiarize flora, fauna, and mineral.

F. L.

"I don't understand, yet I press forward."

$\mathcal{F}.\ \mathcal{L}.$

Seréz Faunantino

Horsemen enter the plain of Megiddo,
riding upon a cloud of carbon and methane.

Stand beside a friend in battle.
Not a foolish battle... lest you be
a fool.

S. F.

The Universe knows what history does not record.

S. F.

Horsemen enter the plain of Megiddo
Riding upon a cloud of carbon and methane
Usher in the beginning of naught
The leader that hastens this time
What shall he be called?
What be his name?
I dare not speak it

Har Megiddo

S. F.

Pile salt on a wound. Another grain
neither heals nor hurts...

S. F.

Posts

...words, images, concepts

My New Year's Resolution is a secret. Oh, alright...
I resolve to be better at keeping secrets.

My clock is slow.
It still tells time.
You just have to do
the math.

My imaginary friends won't shut up.
That's why I can't concentrate.

A BOY'S DILEMMA: Nature vs Nurture

"Dad is schizophrenic and Mom is bipolar.
Which will I be?"

"You don't have to be either. Environment also
plays a role in your development."

"My environment is... Dad is schizophrenic and
Mom is bipolar."

"Oh."

DRUNK BABY SAYS...

"I don't always drink beer. Sometimes I drink Scotch."

HE IS, THE MOST INTERESTING BABY IN THE WORLD.

DRUNK BABY SAYS...

"I don't always drink with Dad. But when I do, Mom makes him sleep on the couch."

HE IS, THE MOST INTERESTING BABY IN THE WORLD.

It's official!
I'm a scary Black man.
I spoke to a woman and
she literally ran away.
Lol

N-WORD

If the plantation owner calls the captive slave a "Piece of Shit", should the captive slave then turn to his children and call them "Little Shits"?

"I am not ashamed to serve, but I am not your servant."
~Canaan, Son of Ham (Cham)

I wish I could say
But I can't
The hardest thing to be
Unsaid

> *writer's block*
> *when one lives to write*

Coda

Thoughtful finale... Now take a bow.

It was the night before one of the cuts
I couldn't sleep for the beeps
And the ch-shh ch-shh
And the intrusive vampire phlebotomist

I heard Karin through a shadow
Clear as crystal in daylight
She whispered, "Jerry"
I asked why she whispered
She said, "The others are already telling me to keep it down."

And she was gone
Back into the shadow
Clear as crystal in daylight

Whispers in Crystal

I sent you a message
Lookin' for your reply
I hit refresh
Refresh...
Internet disconnect
There's a storm
Out in the world, Sis
You should be here with me, Sis
Help me make sense
I hit refresh
Refresh...
Internet disconnect
I miss you
You should be here with me
Happy Birthday

1: 47 am 09 20 2016
Refresh...

No mind world below
Paradise hangs before you
Life is death is life

Karin's Haiku

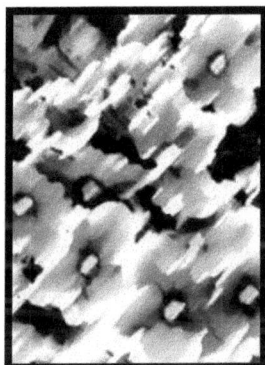

Thank you for reading
Lovely Faze.
Look for a new title in 2019.
Sincerely,

Owen Patterson